A Gonzalo Roig

CORDOBA

From the Spanish Suite "ANDALUCIA"

By ERNESTO LECUONA

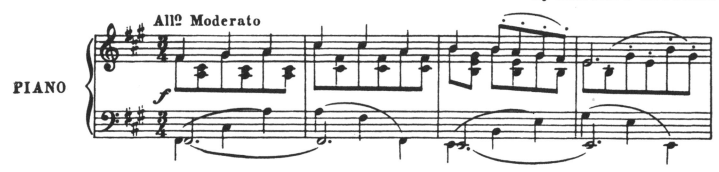

M 3

A Doris Niles

"ANDALUCIA"
From the Spanish Suite "ANDALUCIA"

By ERNESTO LECUONA

Allegro Vivace

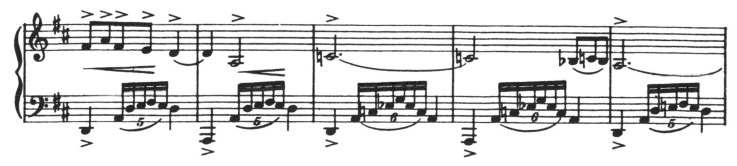

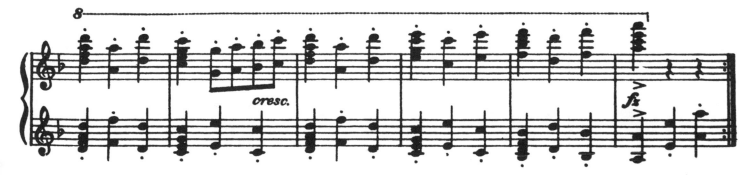

A Pablo Luna

ALHAMBRA

From the Spanish Suite "ANDALUCIA"

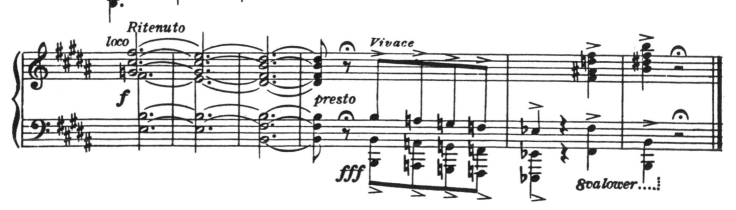

GITANERIAS

By ERNESTO LECUONA

Presto

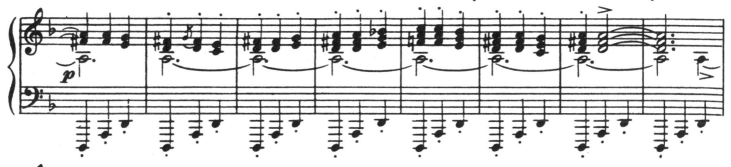

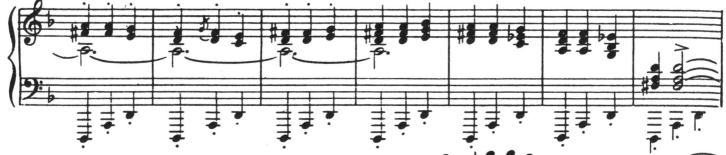

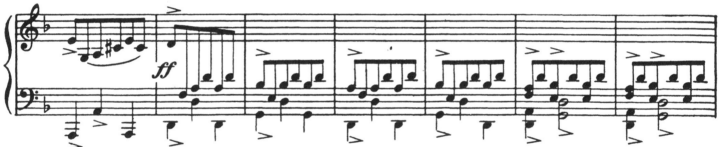

GUADALQUIVIR

From the Spanish Suite "ANDALUCIA" By ERNESTO LECUONA

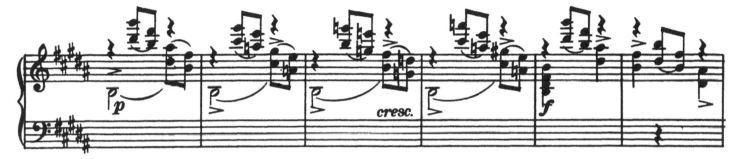

To Hubert De Blanck

MALAGUEŇA

from the Spanish Suite "Andalucia"

by ERNESTO LECUONA

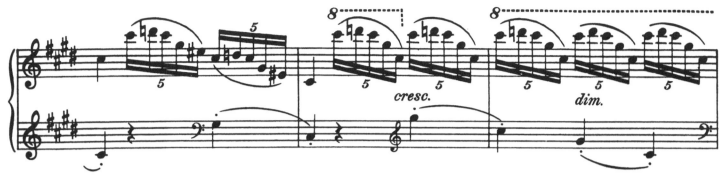

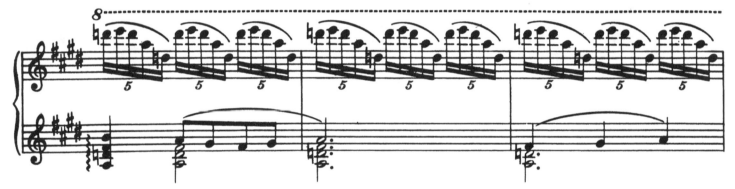

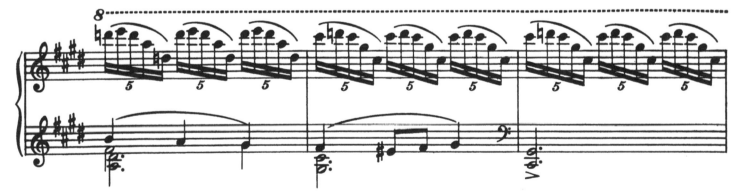

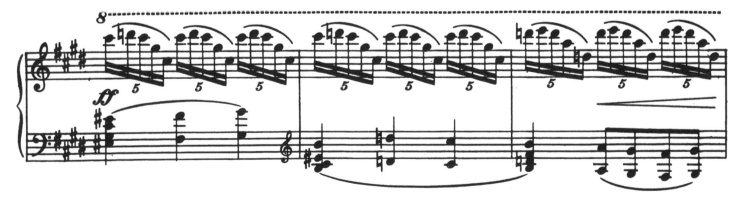

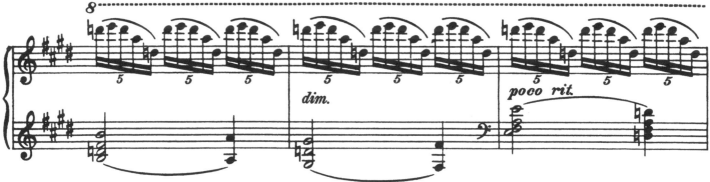

accel.   poco   a   poco

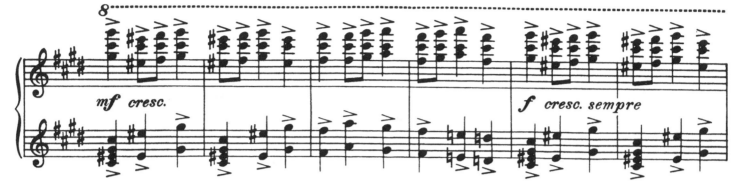

Vivace

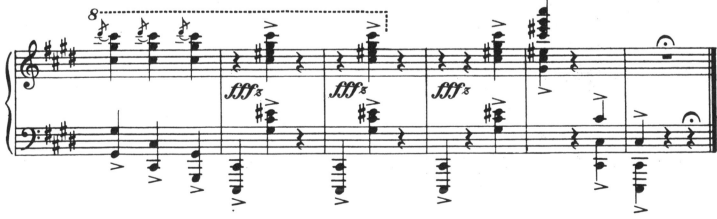